SOUTHWOLD
TO
ALDEBURGH
IN OLD PHOTOGRAPHS

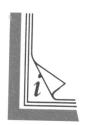

SOUTHWOLD
TO
ALDEBURGH
IN OLD PHOTOGRAPHS

COMPILED BY
HUMPHREY PHELPS

ALAN SUTTON

Alan Sutton Publishing Limited
Phoenix Mill · Far Thrupp · Stroud · Gloucestershire

First Published 1991

British Library Cataloguing in Publication Data

Southwold to Aldeburgh in old photographs.
I. Phelps, Humphrey
942.64

ISBN 0–86299–900–6

Typeset in 9/10 Korinna.
Typesetting and origination by
Alan Sutton Publishing Limited.
Printed in Great Britain by
The Bath Press, Avon.

CONTENTS

INTRODUCTION

It is more than thirty years since first my wife and I saw and immediately fell in love with the part of Suffolk between Southwold and Aldeburgh. We were enchanted by all the greens at Southwold and the magnificent church with sunlight streaming through its clear glass windows. There is no sunlight quite like that of Southwold, and when dusk had fallen the moon shone on the sea like a stairway to the heavens. On nights when the moon was not shining the lighthouse cast its intermittent glow upon the town. There was the sight and sound and smell of the sea, and air redolent of beer being brewed. Perched high above the water, Southwold had a buoyancy to match its skies.

At tiny Blythburgh the huge church stands as evidence of the former size of the village. Our journey continued to Walberswick and on to dear, desolate, deserted Dunwich which cast its spell upon us, a spell which has grown stronger with the passing years. Dunwich itself though has become smaller through the centuries, having lost so much to the sea. Had it not lost so much it might have been a thriving port today, its surrounds a conglomeration of warehouses, factories and houses, a different place altogether from the Dunwich we know now, but not a place to draw us with its magical spell. We went on to Dunwich Heath, Westleton Heath, Westleton village with its large green and thatched church, Middleton, which can so easily be missed by strangers, and another thatched church at Theberton. Leiston is quite different and lacks the charm of other places on the route. It was an industrial town where Garrett's once made steam traction engines. But who can be fascinated by steam engines and fail to pay some regard to a town where they were made? Thorpeness must be seen to be believed and Friston still has a windmill. And so to Aldeburgh. Aldeburgh is quite different from Southwold where you look down to the sea. At Aldeburgh there is the illusion of looking up at a sea that threatens to engulf the town, and has done so on occasion. To this stretch of Suffolk we have returned year after year.

The book is divided into sections, each of the larger towns having a section to itself. There are also sections on the sea, the land and on windmills. Looking at these photographs it is easy to become nostalgic but we should remember that the period covered by them was a hard time for many people and wages and conditions were often appalling. Men lost their lives at sea, the fishing industry declined, farming suffered a long depression and there were two World Wars.

Yet much has been lost which was of value. Once nearly all these places provided a livelihood for their inhabitants, either from the sea, the land or related trades. The Garrett Works at Leiston drew upon a work force from Walberswick to

Aldeburgh and its products were renowned the world over, but the Garrett Works are no more. The fishing industry has lost its former importance and the land no longer provides much employment either directly or indirectly. The windmills no longer turn and few still stand.

The villages look trim and the houses are colour washed and roofed with beautiful pantiles, but because few of them house people who work in the locality the former vitality and close-knit communities no longer exist. In the time following the period covered by these photographs there have been great changes. Modern agriculturalists, those who know so much but not enough to realize how little they know, have altered the landscape. Farming has ceased to be husbandry and has become an industry. A way of life, the work of generations and the rural structure have been destroyed. Fortunately, this part of Suffolk has escaped much of the attention of these 'improvers'. Suffolk has also produced three fine breeds of farm livestock – the Suffolk Punch, the Red Poll, and Suffolk Sheep – four if the Large Black Pig is included. But only the Suffolk Sheep is a major breed today. The horse was ousted by the tractor, the cow and the pig by fashion and specialization.

Study the windmills and imagine what a wonderful sight they must have been, towering above village, farm and field. Reflect on the bustle at the harbours and the fishing villages. Or look at the clothes people were wearing. How varied and lively were these folk despite the hardships many endured! These are the people who made this district, but they had a lot of help from the sea and the soil which are still with us, together with those high skies and that luminous light, the delight not only of artists.

Thirty years ago the distinctive Suffolk accent could be heard everywhere, in the fields, on the beaches, in the villages and streets and the public houses. Now hardly a man can be seen in the fields. Around the fishing boats on the shore the accent can still be heard but elsewhere it is becoming increasingly rare.

This is where I have been fortunate. One of the many pleasures of this book for me is that it has taken me to the homes of real Suffolk people, to meet those, or their descendants, who have made this part of the county. And when they spoke I heard the authentic Suffolk voice, which is music to my ears. The book may have other bonuses. I hope it will make local inhabitants and visitors alike, after looking at these photographs, more determined that this delectable land and seascape is not despoiled, and that it will encourage people to treasure their old photographs. Today's snapshots will be somebody else's old photographs tomorrow.

One pleasure remains, and that is to thank those people who have been so generous and trusting in lending me their photographs, in imparting their knowledge and inviting me into their homes. In a sense it has made me feel that I belong to this enchanting district. Home, they say, is where the heart is, and part of mine has been here for more than thirty years.

SECTION ONE

Southwold

The sun over the rim of the world greets us before anyone else, and the evening skies, each evening new and unrepeatable, strike sparks from the church tower, the river below the Common, and the lighthouse behind us.

John Burke

THE ENTRANCE TO SOUTHWOLD COMMON, taken from a glass plate negative. The lighthouse was not built until the 1890s.

LOOKING UP THE HIGH STREET FROM THE MARKET PLACE, the pump in the centre. The ancient Market Cross which stood here was sold for £39 and removed in 1809. The Swan Hotel, left, was first licensed in 1763. Parson Woodforde stayed at the hotel in 1786 but was unimpressed with it and with Southwold. Winston Churchill came to stay at the Swan on 21 June 1940, soon after he became Prime Minister.

BATHING HUTS ON THE BEACH, C. 1908. The huts were owned by Smith & Palmer. In an essay on Southwold Adrian Bell wrote, 'The sunlit sea is like an angel, glittering and breathing.'

DENNY & SON, TAILORS, Lorne Road, c. 1890. The business was established in 1850. Mr Frederick Denny is in the doorway. (See pp. 22 and 23.)

NORTH PARADE, LOOKING TOWARDS EAST CLIFF, with the coastguard lookout on the right, c. 1900. Locally, this spot was known as Cuddy Corner.

EAST CLIFF. The Sailors' Reading Room is on East Cliff and contains photographs, paintings and sketches. It is open to the public.

THE PIER with the *Belle* steamer, July 1924. The pier was built in 1900. Its head was lost following damage by storms in 1934. It suffered further damage during the war and again later.

HIGH STREET, 1900. On 25 April 1659 a fire, heightened by a violent wind, destroyed the town hall, market house, market place, prison, granaries, shops, warehouses and 238 dwelling houses and other buildings, all within four hours. Goods, nets and tackle, and all the fish, corn, malt, barley and coal in the town were destroyed.

CONSTITUTIONAL HILL, looking towards the town.

THE KING'S HEAD, 1910. The King's Head was first granted a licence in 1743.

MARLBOROUGH HOTEL, 1905. This stood on the front, near the present Craighurst, and was completely destroyed by a direct hit in the bombing raid of 15 May 1943. The church was hit in the same raid. During the war thirteen civilians were killed and seventy-seven properties were destroyed or damaged by raids. In July 1940 Southwold was evacuated and its civilian population reduced by two-thirds. The town became a restricted area and no visitors were allowed. Naval guns were placed on Gun Hill and at the Harbour, where a hole was blown in a pier; the railway bridge was also blown up for defence. There were tank traps and defence works around the town, spiked girders on the beach and minefields in the sea.

THE GRAND HOTEL. This used to stand opposite the pier. It was built by the East Coast Development Company which also built the pier, the Pier Avenue road and laid out the gardens along the front. During the Second World War it was requisitioned by the military and later demolished.

FUND RAISING in the Market Place during the First World War.

HIGH STREET, September 1914. Southwold's farewell to its National Reservists.

WAITING FOR NEWS OF THE WAR outside Chapmans the newsagent in High Street. This was taken during the First World War.

LIFEBOAT DAY, before 1914. The lifeboat is being towed along North Parade by brewery horses.

A MOTOR BUS IN HIGH STREET, 1906.

SOUTHWOLD ROVERS, 1925. Eric Tooke holds the Southwold Hospital Cup.

THE DUKE OF YORK ON THE COMMON. The Duke of York, who became King George VI in 1937, visited Southwold every August from 1931 to 1938 for the Duke of York's Camp, which took boys from factories and public schools. An earlier Duke of York also stayed in Southwold. When the Dutch were preparing an attack upon England in 1672, James, Duke of York, (later James II), High Admiral of the Fleet, made Southwold his headquarters. That year the Battle of Sole Bay took place.

HIGH STREET, 1953, decorated for the coronation of Queen Elizabeth II.

DENNY & SON, Market Place, 1898. The business moved from Lorne Road to the Market Place in 1895. Canova's is on the left. Mrs Canova was a very large lady and when she died a crane was used to remove her from the bedroom. On occasions footsteps have been heard in an upstairs room of Denny & Son's premises but, on investigation, the room has always been found to be unoccupied. A ghost is reputed to walk in Child's Yard, adjacent to the premises.

DENNY & SON, Market Place, 1901, the year a new shop-front was fitted at a total cost of £260.

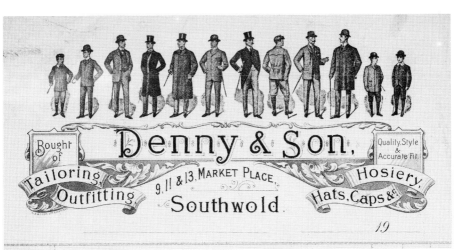

Bought of

Tailoring, Outfitting, 9, 11 & 13, MARKET PLACE, Southwold.

Denny & Son,

Quality. Style & Accurate Fit.

Hosiery, Hats, Caps &c.

THIS OLD-ESTABLISHED AND RESPECTED BUSINESS has had many distinguished customers, among whom have been Sir Alfred Munnings, the artist, Adrian Bell, the author, and George Orwell. Orwell lived in Southwold during the 1930s and continued to have his suits made by Denny's after he left.

THE SOLE BAY BREWERY, 1872. The brewery appears to have evolved from the old brewhouse at the back of the Swan and dates from 1641. The name Adnams was first associated with the brewery in 1872.

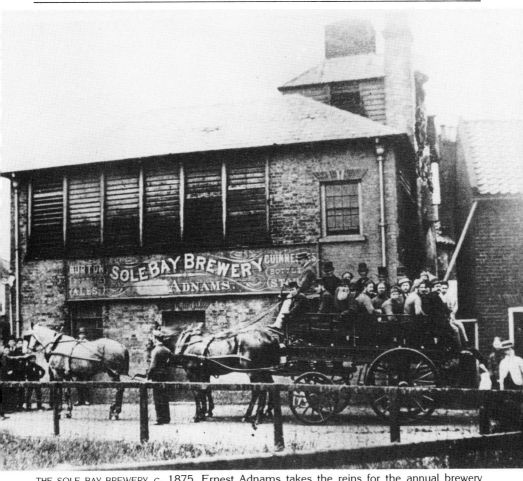

THE SOLE BAY BREWERY, C. 1875. Ernest Adnams takes the reins for the annual brewery outing, with the entire work force, which includes one man wearing a stove-pipe hat, sitting behind him. Today the brewery employs 130 people.

ADNAMS & CO. LTD, SOLE BAY BREWERY, C. 1920s. Since the time of the last photograph the brewery has prospered and expanded and taken over three other breweries. Then, as now, its success was based on producing excellent traditional beer, using only the finest ingredients, barley from East Anglia and hops from Kent. The liquor (water) used to come from a fresh water spring half a mile out to sea but this was damaged during the Second World War. The strain of yeast has not changed since 1943. Today the beer is famous far beyond the county of Suffolk and has gained many awards. Brewers once used the slogan 'Beer is Best'. Adnams could justly claim that theirs is the best of the best.

'TALLY HO' is Adnams' strong beer, first brewed c. 1880. Today it is available in bottles. Bitter, Mild (a dark traditional country brew) and Extra are available on draught. In 1904 'Tally Ho' was two shillings per gallon; Best Bitter, one shilling and sixpence; Mild, one shilling. In 1970 the brewery returned to using horses for local deliveries. Resisting takeover efforts successfully, the brewery is still independent and has seventy houses, some of which once had smuggling connections. Happily, our route from Southwold to Aldeburgh is lined with its houses. This illustration is from 1891.

SOUTHWOLD STATION in its heyday.

SOUTHWOLD RAILWAY STATION, before 1914. The Southwold Railway ran from Southwold to Halesworth with an intermediate station at Wenhaston. Later there were stations at Blythburgh and Walberswick. The line had a 3 ft gauge. Construction started in May 1878 and the railway opened in September 1879. The Board of Trade imposed a 16 m.p.h. speed limit. By 1900 more than 100,000 passengers were using the line and 15,000 tons of freight were being carried annually. In 1914 a mile-long branch line to the Harbour was opened. The railway operated at a profit until 1926 when it made its first loss. The last passenger train ran on 11 April 1929 and the final freight train a week later.

THE SOUTHWOLD RAILWAY – WAITING AT THE TERMINUS FOR THE DOWN EXPRESS WHICH IS SOMEWHAT LATE - A VERY UNUSUAL OCCURRENCE.

ONE IN A SERIES OF CARICATURES OF THE SOUTHWOLD RAILWAY, drawn by Reg Carter who can be seen by the station sign. The carriage from the Swan met every train.

THE INTERIOR OF A CARRIAGE on the Southwold Railway, c. 1908. In 1879 the railway stock consisted of three engines, six carriages and six trucks. By the time the line closed another engine and thirty trucks had been added. The railway's peak period was 1912–13. There were four trains each way daily. Cheap excursion tickets were issued from Mondays to Fridays. A first-class return from Southwold to Halesworth cost two shillings and third-class, one shilling.

A SOUTHWOLD TRAIN CROSSING THE RIVER BLYTH. An early photograph showing the original swing bridge.

THE SOUTHWOLD EXPRESS – THE BRIDGE IS UNABLE TO STAND THE STRAIN OF THE ANNUAL EXCURSION TRAIN – LUCKILY THE LIFEBOAT IS NEAR AND ALL ARE SAVED

A SOUTHWOLD TRAIN ON THE BRIDGE OVER THE RIVER BLYTH, as seen by Reg Carter (who had the grace to apologize to all for this and other libels of the Southwold line).

Blythburgh, Walberswick, Dunwich

I defy anyone, at desolate, exquisite Dunwich, to be disappointed in anything. The minor key is struck here with a felicity that leaves no sigh to be breathed, no loss to be suffered ...

Henry James

THE GREEN, Blythburgh. The house was originally two cottages.

Old Forge, Blythburgh

THE FORGE at Blythburgh, c. 1920, with Messrs Goodwin and Parkinson, a horse-drawn
mowing machine and zig-zag harrows. The blacksmith is popularly associated with the
shoeing of horses, but he served the community in many other ways. Products of the smithy
included hand-forged nails and a variety of tools. By the 1920s much of the work would
have involved the repair of agricultural implements.

A BLACKSMITH at Blythburgh, 1912.

LONDON ROAD, Blythburgh, c. 1905.

MILKING TIME AT UNION FARM, Bulcamp, c. 1935. Newton Rose is on the right. There are pails and three-legged stools for hand milkers.

CHURCH FARM, Blythburgh, c. 1910. Archie Kett and his younger brother with horse and tumbril.

THE SOUTHWOLD–WALBERSWICK FERRY across the River Blyth, 1907, looking towards Walberswick. Mr Cross is in charge. By this time Walberswick had become home to a colony of artists. Principal among them was Philip Wilson Steer who painted many scenes of the village.

WALBERSWICK FERRY, 1916. The River Blyth Ferry Company was formed in 1885 and worked between Walberswick and Southwold until 1942. A chain ferry was in operation sometime in the nineteenth century; previously the ferry had consisted of two boats. The River Blyth Ferry Company operated a steam ferry. In the background, left of the ferry, is the water tower on Southwold Common which had a windmill to pump the water.

WALBERSWICK FERRY. By the 1920s the ferry had a boat (built on Southwold Common) large enough to take a horse and cart; it was powered by a donkey engine. The next boat was larger still and had a tall funnel.

THE FERRY, C. 1936.

THESE PERFORMING ELEPHANTS arrived at Darsham Station *en route* to Southwold via Walberswick. At the ferry they would not part and went on board together, almost sinking the ferry boat.

SCOTS FISH GIRLS rowing back to Walberswick from Southwold, 1908. Herring and sprat curing was done on a large scale at Southwold in 1908, and during the season some Scots fish girls lodged at Walberswick.

PULLING TO SEA at Walberswick due to lack of wind, c. 1900.

PLANTING MARRAN GRASS after east coast floods in 1953.

WALBERSWICK STATION.

SOUTHWOLD RAILWAY. The Heronry, between Blythburgh and Walberswick.

THE SOUTHWOLD EXPRESS - THE GUARD AS A PROFITABLE SIDELINE - PUTS THE DINNERS OF THE COTTAGERS ALONG THE ROUTE · ON THE UP TRAIN - THESE BEING DONE TO PERFECTION BY THE RETURN JOURNEY · THE PROCESS OF CURING THE RENOWNED SOUTHWOLD BLOATERS IS SHEWN

SOUTHWOLD RAILWAY as seen by Reg Carter, who is sitting on the step of the first carriage.

JOHN SMITH WITH DONKEY, 1910. This is the fourth church on this site. William Dowsing, appointed Parliamentary visitor to the churches of Suffolk during the Civil War in 1643, played havoc with the church at Walberswick. He destroyed forty windows and defaced all the tombs.

WALBERSWICK VILLAGE SCHOOL, 1879, with headmistress Miss Alice Friend. The school is now the Parish Lantern Craft and Tea Rooms.

NEW WALBERSWICK SCHOOL, 1948. The headmistress is Mrs Hargreaves. Philip Kett is in the middle row, third from left. The school closed in 1976.

WALBERSWICK VILLAGE STREET. The timbered house in the background, called Mercers Hall, was brought from Lavenham in 1907 and rebuilt here. Several houses were brought to Walberswick and rebuilt.

OLD ANCHOR INN, 1908. It was later dismantled, taken by builder's barrow along the street and rebuilt at a cost of £40. It is now called Anchor Lea.

NEW ANCHOR INN, 1937. Far right is Mr 'Weary' Page who used to build longshore fishing boats single-handed.

THE PRIVATE CINEMA at Walberswick. It had forty-eight seats but closed in 1949.

WALBERSWICK CINEMA.

THE WATER MILL ON WESTWOOD MARSHES, 1930s. It was built c. 1700 and used until 1939. The military then used it for target practice. It was burnt down in the 1960s. Westwood Marshes was the site of an army training camp during the First World War. In the Second World War the marshes were deliberately flooded as an obstacle to invasion.

ST JAMES STREET, Dunwich. The cottage, extreme right, was pulled down in 1869 and replaced by a cottage which is now the museum. The Museum was formerly housed in the old Rocket House, but that closed in 1965. The Museum opened on its present site in 1972. By the wall is a Dunwich rose. To attempt to understand Dunwich a visit to the Museum is essential. A model of medieval Dunwich shows the size the village once was, and how much of it has been lost to the sea. Dunwich was once the capital of East Anglia and the See of a Bishop.

THE ROAD INTO DUNWICH FROM BLYTHBURGH with the River Dun. A bridge was put over the river in 1939. St James' church, built in 1830, is in the background. Troops were stationed at Dunwich during both World Wars. In the Second World War Dunwich became a restricted area. 'Dragons Teeth', a Second World War defence measure, can still sometimes be seen on the beach at low water. Edward Fitzgerald was a frequent visitor to Dunwich. On 2 July 1878 he wrote, 'I have taken that single little lodging at Dunwich for the next three months, and shall soon be under those priory walls again. But the poor little Dunwich rose, brought by those monks from the North Country, will have passed after the hot weather we are at last having.' Carlyle came in 1855, Swinburne in 1875 and '77, and Jerome K. Jerome was a frequent visitor.

RUINS OF GREYFRIARS PRIORY, C. 1890. The Grey Friars came to Dunwich in 1290. After the dissolution the Priory was used for various secular purposes, among them the town gaol. The cattle on the right are Red Polls, the native Suffolk breed.

A CATHOLIC PROCESSION, C. 1923. Dunwich was never a place of pilgrimage but local Catholics started one to St Felix and St Edmund between the wars.

DUNWICH VILLAGE SCHOOL in the early 1900s.

There blooms the heath, whose bright, though humble flower,
An emblem shows of modest beauty's power;
There smiles the Dunwich Rose, with snow-like blossom,
Soft, pure, and white, as in the cygnet's bosom:
This decks the stern and sterile cliff, and throws
O'er the rough brow new beauty where it grows,
Gives the proud ruggedness an aspect fair,
Like hope that brightens on the brow of care!

(The Dunwich Rose – *James Bird*)

DUNWICH CRICKET TEAM AND SUPPORTERS in 1903. Henry James, another visitor to Dunwich wrote, 'The biggest items are of course the two ruins, the great church and its tall tower, now quite on the verge of the cliff, and the crumbled, ivied wall of the immense cincture of the Priory. These things have parted with almost every grace, but they still keep up the work that they have been engaged in for centuries and that cannot be better described than as adding mystery to mystery ... The mystery sounds for ever in the hard, straight tide, and hangs, through the long still summer days and over the low diked fields, in the soft, thick light.'

REMAINS OF ALL SAINTS' CHURCH, Dunwich, 1905. The medieval church was forty-three metres long. The ruins started going into the sea in 1903.

THE REMAINS OF ALL SAINTS' in 1912; the last part of the church disappeared into the sea in 1919. Dunwich had lost at least seven churches to the sea before All Saints' went, two in the thirteenth century, two in the fourteenth, one in the fifteenth, one in the sixteenth and one in the eighteenth century. The Blackfriars Monastery was lost to the sea in the fourteenth century. The sites of two hospitals remain.

THE BARNE ARMS, 1947, formerly the Ship. The Ship Inn began in the sixteenth century. Its name changed to the Barne Arms over 100 years ago but reverted to its proper name in 1967. The Barne family had been merchants in the City of London, the East India Company and the Muscovy Company, and had been in Suffolk from the early eighteenth century, buying an estate at Sotterley in 1744. Dunwich attracted them because, although the population was small, it returned two members to Parliament (see *Dunwich – The Rotten Borough* by Dr O. G. Pickard, published by the Trustees of Dunwich Museum). The Barne family acquired the Dunwich estate in 1754.

> *Poor Mr Barne! The thankless crew!*
> *It was a dirty thing to do!*
> *They've turned your pub into the Ship*
> *And shot you on the rubbish tip.*
>
> *(from* Dunwich Revisited *– Oliver Rooke)*

A SALE NOTICE of Dunwich estate, 1947. (This, the previous and the next three photographs are part of a series taken when the estate was put up for auction.) Mr W. C. Westliage, a Dunwich inhabitant, studies the notice.

MR CLARK, ANOTHER DUNWICH MAN, seems to be thinking about the auction of the village which will include his house.

THE PRINCIPAL RESIDENCE in Dunwich, known as Greyfriars, home of the Barne family. Lord Dawson of Penn spent much of his time here.

THE DUNWICH VILLAGE SCHOOL in 1947. The lot number in the forthcoming auction is above the doorway. The school closed in 1964 and the building is now a private house.

At the Dunwich Estate Sale of 1947 (auctioneers Jackson-Stops & Staff) there were fifty-one lots including four farms. Some of the prices realized were: Cliff House with twenty-eight acres, £6,250; Greyfriars, £7,750; Greyfriars Monastery, £850; the General Stores, £525; the School House, £450; the School, £510; the Old Post Office, £460; the Old Town Hall, £400; the Barne Arms and the Red House were withdrawn. Total for the estate sold, £54,385.

Westleton, Middleton-cum-Fordley, Theberton

No scent like the breeze over Westleton Heath,
Making sport with the thistle-down showers;
It has gathered the salt of the tide in its breath ...

Alice Cochrane

WESTLETON. The Green, early 1900s. The tall building in the centre is the White Horse Inn.

WESTLETON. The Street, 1930s. Cain & Son, grocers and general stores, is on the right. The business opened on this site in 1885 and closed in January 1990. In 1907 this shop was selling pork at 7d. per lb; a loaf of bread at 2½d.; butter at 1s. 3d. per lb; sugar at 5d. for 2 lb and cheese at 9d. per lb. In 1935 bacon was 1s. 8d. per lb; bib and brace overalls were 3s. 11d. The tall building in the centre was the Primitive Methodist chapel which opened in 1868 and closed during the 1960s.

WESTLETON CHURCH. Note the tower which has now gone. In the 1930s both church and chapel held annual children's outings to the seaside. The church one was to Dunwich and the chapel one to Southwold.

WESTLETON VILLAGE CELEBRATION for Queen Victoria's Diamond Jubilee at Grange Meadow in 1897.

FESTIVAL WEEK AT WESTLETON, August 1951. Every year Westleton had a week-long festival and elected a festival Queen.

EMPIRE DAY, 1912. Westleton schoolchildren and boy scouts.

WESTLETON. A lady at a thatched cottage which is now demolished. A garage now stands on the site.

WESTLETON SCHOOL in the early 1900s. The top of a windmill can just be seen on the far right. The school opened in 1842 and closed in 1965. When a Mr Gladwyn was the schoolmaster the children had a song:

> Mr Gladwyn is a very good man
> He goo to charch on Sunday
> And prays by God to give him strength
> To thash the boys o' Monday.

WESTLETON SCHOOL, 1909.

STEAM ENGINE, YOXFORD ROAD, WESTLETON, at the entrance to what is now called Fisk Yard. The engine is hauling timber.

RACKFORD RUN between Westleton and Middleton in the nineteenth century. There was great rivalry between the two villages and it was here that the youths from the villages met and fought.

THE STREET, Middleton, c. 1927, an unmade road. The cottage with washing hanging out is now demolished and the site is part of the Bell Inn car park.

MIDDLETON CHURCH. The churchyard once contained two churches, one serving Fordley, now no more, and the Middleton one, seen here. Sharing the same churchyard caused hostility between the two parishes due to the sound of each other's church bells. If services in the churches did not coincide, the congregation of one was deafened by the bells of the other. All traces of Fordley church have gone and the villages have merged and become Middleton-cum-Fordley. Middleton church almost went too, as the next photograph shows.

MIDDLETON CHURCH, Friday 14 October 1955. The thatched roof caught fire. The church was restored but no longer has a thatched roof.

MIDDLETON BRASS BAND in the school yard in 1889.

PUPILS AT MIDDLETON SCHOOL, 13 October 1910.

MIDDLETON SCHOOL GARDENING CLASS, May 1917. The school allotments were on Back Hill. Miss Carpenter, headmistress, is third from right.

A WEDDING GROUP outside Vine Cottage, Middleton in 1935.

RECTORY ROAD. Fordley had a rectory, Middleton a vicarage. Around the turn of the century baptisms took place in a pond on Middleton Moor. The ceremony was conducted by two women who hired a cottage at Yoxford and visited the surrounding district. These two 'No Sect' preachers also held open-air meetings.

MIDDLETON VILLAGE OUTING to Dunwich, 22 August 1879.

THE BLACKSMITH'S SHOP, Theberton, *c.* 1938. Mr J. Coates, who later became landlord at the Red Lion, is on the other side of the road. Mr Coates used to ring all five bells at once at Theberton church, one rope in each hand, one from each elbow and one on his foot.

THE GISSING FAMILY GROUP, Theberton, early 1900s.

THE STRAFED ZEPPELIN L48 at Theberton, 17 June 1917. The Zeppelin was 600 ft in length, 50 ft in diameter and weighed over 20 tons. On 17 June 1917 at 2 a.m. the Zeppelin came in at Orfordness, rounded Wickham Market, went past Woodbridge, dropped bombs near Martlesham and was then engaged by AA guns. Lieut. L. P. Watkins of 37 Squadron went up from Goldhanger and fired two drums into her tail, then three further bursts and the Zeppelin exploded into flames. The fall took about five minutes. The airship came down stern first, smashing the whole afterpart, and the front gondola was badly damaged. Three members of the crew survived but the other sixteen were killed. They were buried in Theberton churchyard.

REMAINS OF THE ZEPPELIN being inspected and guarded.

THEBERTON QUOITS TEAM, 1946. This is an outdoor game. The quoits are of steel, approximately 7 lb in weight and 7 in in diameter; the pitch is 18 or 21 yd. The game is played in teams of six to a score of 33.

MR AND MRS COATES' WEDDING, C. 1900.

THE EEL'S FOOT, Eastbridge, c. 1945. The Eel's Foot had a tradition of country singing. At one time it also had smuggling associations. On 11 December 1747 the Revenue men called in the assistance of soldiers, but the smugglers caused them to retreat – to the Eel's Foot. The soldiers were enjoying themselves there when the smugglers arrived and opened fire.

Saxmundham and Peasenhall

And faithful Suffolk,
Sweet with sleepy space.

A. E. Tomlinson

SAXMUNDHAM. South entrance from High Street.

SAXMUNDHAM. Market Street, 1900.

SAXMUNDHAM. High Street, 1900. The Bell is on the right. In 1842 a company rebuilt the Bell at the cost of £11,000 and erected a Corn Exchange and Public Room. During the nineteenth century Saxmundham had a large corn market every Thursday, a fair for toys and paddlery on Whit Tuesdays and a hiring fair for servants at Old Michaelmas.

SAXMUNDHAM HIGH STREET.

SAXMUNDHAM HIGH STREET. Most of Saxmundham is the High Street.

The Wrench Series No. 4128

YOXFORD. The Three Tuns Hotel, burnt down in January 1925. It was reputed to have Nelson's and Dickens's names in its visitors book. On the opposite side of the road it had a flower garden which may have been why Yoxford was called the Garden of Suffolk. It was rebuilt and named The Griffin.

PEASENHALL, at the bottom end of The Street. This is thought to be celebrations for the coronation of King George V in 1910. The village band is leading the procession. In 1843 Peasenhall had two families making seed drills, three blacksmiths, three shoemakers, three wheelwrights, two carpenters, a harness maker, a cooper, a straw hat maker, a corn merchant and miller, a tailor, a maltster and a farrier. By the time of this photograph one drill maker – Smyth – was known throughout the UK and the continent.

A SMYTH & SONS CORN DRILL. Peasenhall was famous for its Smyth corn drills. James Smyth, a young wheelwright in Peasenhall early in the nineteenth century, invented an improved corn drill which contained levers and swing steerage. The machines were exhibited at various markets together with an offer to do contract drilling at two shillings and sixpence per acre. The firm prospered and soon Smyth Drills were being used all over the country and exported to the continent.

JAMES SMYTH & SONS. A poster of 1900.

THE INTERIOR OF THE SMYTH DRILL WORKS. The works were close to the church. The firm was still flourishing in the 1940s but closed in the late 1960s. The Peasenhall village sign depicts a Smyth drill.

MR HUNT, C. 1890, a cooper who worked in a barn in Bruisyard Road. The barn has now collapsed.

MR NEWSOME AT HIS HARNESS SHOP in The Street, Peasenhall, c. 1930.

LOTTIE PEPPER, with a very elegant peram-
bulator, by Sibton Abbey House in the
early 1920s. Sibton, which adjoins Peasenhall, had the only Cistercian house in
Suffolk. The Sibton village sign depicts two
Cistercian monks.

A COTTAGE IN THE STREET, Peasenhall, as it was when William Gardiner lived in it. William Gardiner was a skilled worker at the Smyth Drill works, a married man and a leading Methodist in the district. His name had been scandalously linked with that of Miss Rose Harsent, a girl who lived in at the nearby Providence House. One early morning in 1902 Rose Harsent was found dead, lying in blood. Gardiner was arrested and twice stood on trial but was neither convicted nor cleared. On his release he left Peasenhall. The murder still attracts attention today. Several books have been written about the murder and at least two novels have been based upon it. The latest and fullest account is *The Peasenhall Murder* by Martin Fido and Keith Skinner, published by Alan Sutton Publishing in 1990.

A SHOOTING PARTY at Peasenhall. The late Mr Gilbert Jerrey is in the centre with a gun on his shoulder. Mr Jerrey was the proprietor of Emmett's Stores in The Street, Peasenhall. Emmett's Stores is still there and a Mr Jerrey is still the proprietor. The shop is renowned for its Suffolk cured bacon and hams and a fine example of an old and genuine village stores.

EMMETT'S STORES.

KELSALE VILLAGE.

KELSALE STREET.

SECTION FIVE

Leiston

Garrett's of Leiston,
Leiston of Garrett's.

HIGH STREET, LEISTON, C. 1906. Leiston was a village that developed into a town as the Garrett Works grew following its establishment in 1778. At that time Leiston's population was only 750. In the nineteenth century it became an industrial town. It was the largest employment centre in the area covered by this book. It drew its work force from an area bounded by Walberswick and Aldeburgh. By the early years of the twentieth century Garrett's were employing over 1,000 people and the Town Works were quite unable to meet the demands of production.

HIGH STREET, LEISTON, c. 1906. The men in this photograph are workers at the Garrett Works. Note the Eton collars on the schoolboys.

LEISTON CORK CLUB, 1913. The members are about to board the carriages for 'an outing'. The members carried 'corks' – ordinary corks decorated with a fancy nail at each end. When one member met another he said 'Cork up!' Failure to produce the cork resulted in a forfeit. Woodbridge also had a Cork Club.

LEISTON RAILWAY STATION. A branch line of the East Suffolk Railway arrived in 1859. It was axed by Beeching. As the Suffolk-born Dowsing was to churches (see p. 41), Beeching was to railways. The new Garrett Works were built by this station.

CHEAPSIDE, LEISTON, c. 1947.

HIGH STREET, LEISTON.

LEISTON FEMALE FOOTBALLERS, 1917. Left, Gertie Rook; centre, Ruby Meadows; right, unknown.

LEISTON WORKS FIRE BRIGADE, November 1913. This fire brigade also served the town and surrounding villages.

TEATIME AT LEISTON BOTTOM WORKS. Children used to bring tea for the workers.

A GROUP OF WORKERS FROM THE BOILER SHOP.

SOME OF GARRETT'S WORK FORCE.

THE SMITHY TUG-OF-WAR TEAM, 1910.

LEISTON ST MARGARETS FC, 1933/4, winners of the Leiston & District League II.

WOMEN OPERATORS AT GARRETT'S, 1916.

MUNITION WORKERS IN THE FIRST WORLD WAR. Left to right: E. Whiting, Mrs Kemp, L. Wildman, P. Barrell. The Station Works accommodated the wood-working department and the foundry. During the First World War it was used for the production of shells and aircraft.

MACHINE SHOP, TOP WORKS, 1930s. By 1846 Garrett's were producing a wide range of agricultural machinery including chaff cutters, grinding mills, oilseed cake crushers, root pulpers, seed drills and threshing machines. At the 'Royal' at Cambridge in 1841 only two threshing machines completed the trials, those made by Garrett's of Leiston and Ransome and May of Ipswich. The following year Garrett's received the award for the best threshing machine. At the 1853 Royal Show Garrett's triumphed again, this time with the best reaping machine.

FITTING SHOP, TOP WORKS, 1930s. In 1851 Garrett's employed 300 men and had a large stand at the Great Exhibition at the Crystal Palace. They were making steam engines for factories, sawmills and farms as well as building their own gasworks which eventually supplied the town with gas. In 1915 electricity was being generated at the Station Works.

THRESHING CORN with a Garrett threshing machine driven by a Garrett steam traction engine. At rear is the elevator which took threshed straw to the top of the rick. The corn stack would have been behind the threshing machine.

ERECTING SHOP, TOP WORKS, 1930s. In 1863 the firm was producing traction engines and had introduced its system of steam ploughing.

TURNERY SHOP, BOTTOM WORKS. In the latter half of the nineteenth century almost ninety per cent of Garrett's production was being exported. Garrett's men went to various parts of the world. A Garrett's advertisement of that time reads, 'Experienced man to work in foreign parts, to travel to all parts of the British Empire, the Austro-Hungarian Empire, and all the Russias. Good rates of pay, 3d. an hour at Leiston, 4d. per hour abroad. Some expenses allowed. Man must be sober, honest and very hard working. References essential.'

A GARRETT TRACTOR, single cylinder, built 1916.

A GARRETT NO. 4 TRACTOR, built 1918. By this time the first of many electric vehicles had also been produced. In the late 1920s trolleybuses, diesel tractors and steam wagons were some of the many and varied productions. In 1937 the Richard Garrett Engineering Works Ltd started shell lathe production again (see p. 91). During the Second World War gun mountings, sections for the Mulberry Harbours and radar equipment were manufactured. Bombs fell on the Works but failed to explode. A large airfield was constructed at Leiston and was later handed over to the US Army Air Force. Garretts of Leiston closed down in July 1980.

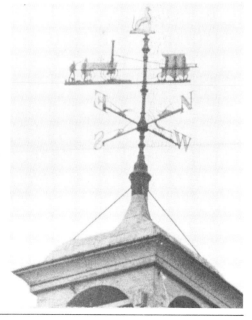

THIS WEATHER VANE stood on top of the Long Shop. The Long Shop, constructed in 1852, is one of the earliest production assembly halls in existence. In 1984 the Long Shop became a museum of artefacts made on the site. The museum features the 200 year history of Garrett's Works and the histories of Leiston and the USAAF 8th Air Base. The weather vane has been returned. The award-winning Long Shop Museum is open from April to October.

SUMMERHILL SCHOOL, LTD., LEISTON, SUFFOLK.

PROSPECTUS.

The principles of this school are given in A. S. Neill's books — "THE PROBLEM CHILD" 1927 : "THE PROBLEM PARENT," 1931 : and "THAT DREADFUL SCHOOL," 1937, all published by Herbert Jenkins, Ltd. Prospective parents should read these books before even thinking of sending a child to Summerhill.

The Fees are from £80 to £160 a year (three Terms), according to age.

New pupils must bring the following with them :—
4 sheets, 4 pillowslips, 4 towels, a rug or eiderdown.
Most pupils have cycles.

Leiston is reachable by the L.N.E.R. from Liverpool Street Station, and the School is opposite the Station. It is two miles from the Sea, and the children bathe there in Summer.

The School has three Tennis Courts and a Hockey Field.

Parents seeking advice about children not at Summerhill, or about to enter Summerhill, pay for interviews.

Parents must give a Term's notice of withdrawal, or pay a Half Term's Fees.

DIRECTORS : A. S. NEILL and MRS. A. S. NEILL.   Telephone Leiston 40.

SUMMERHILL, A. S. Neill's provocatively experimental 'free' or 'dreadful' school. It started in 1924 at a house called Summerhill in Lyme Regis. In 1927 the school moved to a house called Newhaven at Leiston but the name Summerhill was retained. In 1940 the school moved to North Wales and the army took over the house and grounds at Leiston. When the school returned to Leiston in 1945 A. S. Neill found that the army had done 'more damage in that time than my kids had done in twenty-five years.'

SUMMERHILL SCHOOL, Leiston. A. S. Neill said he never regretted coming to Leiston. 'The air is bracing ... I am often asked what the town thinks of us and I never know the answer.'

Friston and Thorpeness

The sky had that luminous clarity which it seems to achieve only in East Anglia.

John Hadfield

SNAPE LANE, FRISTON. William 'Cockeye' Moss, the local thatcher, is in the pony trap. Friston windmill is in the background on the left.

FRISTON. The smithy and travvis which have been demolished. A travvis was the name for an open shed adjoining a blacksmith's shop in which horses were shod. 'To put the smith on the door' is to lock it. The blacksmith's two-handed sledgehammer was called a bout hammer. The poster advertises 'Ye Olde Country Fayre'.

JOHN MOSS. Friston's overseer and parish clerk from 1894. The photograph was taken before 1914.

THE COMMITTEE AND JUDGES at the Furrow Drawing Match at Firs Farm, Friston in the late 1930s. Another kind of Drawing Match, at which the Suffolk Punch excelled, was popular in Suffolk during the eighteenth century. It was a contest of a horse's strength in drawing (pulling) heavy loads.

BILLY LOWE (left) AND BOB WRIGHT, the owner's son, at Friston Mill, where they both worked, in 1936.

FRISTON SCHOOLCHILDREN on the lawn at Friston Hall, May Day, c. 1909.

FRISTON SCHOOL, MIDDLE CLASS, c. 1923.

FRISTON GIRLS' FRIENDLY SOCIETY, 1927.

FRISTON HOME GUARD PLATOON, 1941.

THE SNAPE EXPRESS used to run from a junction between Saxmundham and Wickham Market and made one journey a day to and from Snape Maltings.

THORPENESS GENERAL STORES AND POST OFFICE, 1912. This was the first shop. Thorpe used to be a small fishing hamlet. The hamlet of Aldringham had only about 100 inhabitants before it began to be developed and known as Thorpeness. Today, the buildings, to quote John Burke, author of *Suffolk*, 'look old world at first glance . . . olde-worlde at second glance . . . incredible on further contemplation.' The Thorpeness we see today began just before the First World War when G. Stuart Ogilvie began to turn the fishing hamlet into 'a corner of Merrie England.' He continued after the war.

THE HOUSE IN THE CLOUDS AND THE WINDMILL at Thorpeness. The house is a water tower. The windmill originally stood at Aldringham and was moved to Thorpeness around 1922.

LAKESIDE HOUSE AND MERE, constructed c. 1910. The mere is only two feet deep.

A MOTOR CAR OWNED BY THE OGILVIE FAMILY. Note the solid rubber tyres.

THORPENESS HALT, between Saxmundham and Aldeburgh. It was closed by Beeching.

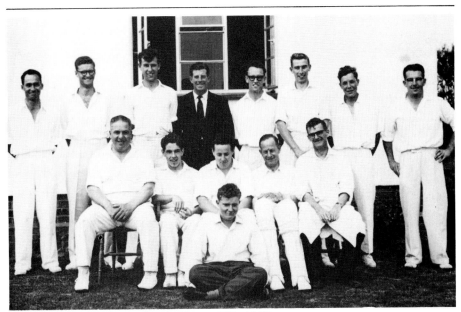

THORPENESS CRICKET TEAM, after the Second World War.

SNAPE WATERING. It was bridged around 1924.

SIZEWELL, 1903. The road from Leiston ending at Hill House. The houses have now been demolished for the nuclear power station.

FRISTON BOY SCOUTS at Sizewell, 1914. They are on beach patrol. Hill House is in the background.

SECTION SEVEN

Aldeburgh

There is no sea like the Aldeburgh sea. It talks to me.

Edward FitzGerald

ALDEBURGH FROM THE SOUTH, 1860, showing the windmill on Fort Green.

MOOT HALL, ALDEBURGH, a sixteenth-century building which was once much further from the sea than it is today. In 1876 the building of a pier by the Moot Hall was started. The first four spans were damaged beyond repair by a sailing barge and the project was abandoned.

GEORGE CRABBE, POET, was born in this house at Slaughden on Christmas Eve 1754. The house has been washed away by the sea. His father was a salt tax collector and George Crabbe eventually became curate of Aldeburgh.

THE OLD CUSTOM HOUSE, built c. 1725. George Crabbe's grandfather, Robert Crabbe, was Comptroller of the Custom House.

HIGH STREET, Aldeburgh, 1894. Earlier in the nineteenth century it was known as The Thoroughfare and had five inns.

HIGH STREET, Aldeburgh, before 1900. In the nineteenth century Aldeburgh became a popular resort. Thomas Carlyle called it 'a beautiful little sea town.'

HIGH STREET, Aldeburgh in the early 1900s. 'Soon as the season comes, and crowds arrive/To their superior rooms the wealthy drive.' The town has two streets running parallel to the shore; it once had three. Only Dunwich has lost more to the sea.

STATION ROAD, Aldeburgh, c. 1912. In the background is the windmill.

THE THREE MARINERS, Slaughden, c. 1910. Over the porch is the shoulder blade of a whale which is now in Aldeburgh Museum. The Three Mariners was deeply involved with smuggling. The inn was called the Anchor in George Crabbe's time. The poet called Slaughden's fishermen 'a bold, artful, surly, savage race.' In 1909 W.A. Dutt described Slaughden as a 'small, sea-threatened cluster of cottages bordering a primitive quay and grouped around an ancient inn with a huge bone of a whale suspended over its front door.' The bone was brought from Iceland by one of the fishing smacks whose crews used to share out the money at the end of the season. The inn was also a meeting place for wildfowlers and poachers. The sea finally washed away the Three Mariners inn soon after this photograph was taken.

SUMMER AT ALDEBURGH, C. 1920. In 1843, according to White's Suffolk Directory, there were 'several convenient bathing machines, and a suite of warm, cold, and shower baths.' To Crabbe the sea was,

Various and vast, sublime in all its forms,
When lulled by zephyrs or when roused by storms,
Its colours changing when from clouds and sun
Shades after shades upon the surface run;
Embrown'd and horrid now and now serene,
In limpid blue and evanescent green.

WINTER AT ALDEBURGH, 5 January 1958, after high tide. The Martello tower is in the distance. Tennyson, who visited Aldeburgh and must have seen what the Aldeburgh sea could do, wrote of . . . 'an ever-breaking shore/That tumbled in the Godless deep.'

WINTER IN THE HIGH STREET, showing the Cottage Hospital which was bombed on 14 December 1942. Two patients were killed and several other people injured.

SUNSET AT ALDEBURGH. 'When skies were poems writ.' (Cecil Lay, who lived at Aldringham.)

THE MARTELLO TOWER after 1953. The Martello tower is to the south of Fort Green. A massive tower battery was erected around 1806 which was intended as a garrison for 100 men. The Martello tower was built a few years later, and was the last to be built.

THE POST OFFICE AND HOUSES DESTROYED BY DELAYED ACTION BOMBS on 14 December 1942.
Four people were killed and three injured in the post office, others were injured elsewhere.
Aldeburgh suffered many bombing raids during the Second World War.

FLOODS IN THE HIGH STREET in 1953. The sea came over the top of the sea defences and
flooded the town. One life was lost.

HAND LAUNDRY GIRLS, C. 1920, at Miss Pettit's Laundry, which was on Fort Green.

ALDEBURGH FIRE BRIDGADE, c. 1896.

ALDEBURGH FOOTBALL TEAM, 1955/6.

ELIZABETH GARRETT ANDERSON (1836–1917) was a daughter of a member of the Garrett family, owners of the Garrett Works at Leiston. She pioneered the right for women to enter the medical profession and became the first female doctor in Britain in 1865. When she became mayor of Aldeburgh in 1908 she was the first female mayor.

BUYING FISH IN THE HIGH STREET, Aldeburgh, 1948. Left to right: Peter Pears, Benjamin Britten, Laurie Baggott, Mrs P. Howard. Benjamin Britten was born at Lowestoft in 1913. In 1937 he made his home in a converted windmill in Snape. In the early summer of 1939 he and Peter Pears went to Canada. In 1942 they returned to Suffolk and two years later Britten started composing the music for *Peter Grimes*, which was inspired by Crabbe's *The Borough*, a poem based on Aldeburgh. The first Aldeburgh Festival, founded by Britten, Pears and Eric Crozier, opened in June 1948. Britten lived in Crabbe Street, Aldeburgh, from 1947 to 1957.

SECTION EIGHT

Sea

The sea – this truth must be confessed – has no generosity. No display of manly qualities – courage, hardihood, endurance, faithfulness – has ever been known to touch its irresponsible consciousness of power.

Joseph Conrad

SOUTHWOLD BEACH, C. 1902. The lighthouse is behind the sails of the fishing boats. There are bathing machines and the pier is in the distance on the right.

FISHING BOATS NEAR GUN HILL, Southwold, c. 1906.

LONGSHORE FISHING BOATS on Southwold beach, c. 1890–1900. Note the capstan-type winch made of wood on the left, in front of the boats. The sails are being allowed to dry. Fisherman had considerable work to do on land as well as at sea.

JAMES CRITTON, boat builder, c. 1900, is on the left. A clinker boat is shown but he also built yawls and gigs. The boat building shed under North Cliff was destroyed by rough seas and storms.

THE BITTERN, returning to Southwold after winning the Lowestoft Regatta Yawl Race in 1903. Built in 1890, the *Bittern* was for many years the fastest boat of this type on this coast. Her nine-foot rudder is now outside the Sailors' Reading Room.

SOUTHWOLD LIFEBOAT. The *Alfred Cory*, a Norfolk and Suffolk clinker boat built by Beeching in 1893, was in use from 1893 to 1918. It was 44 ft long, 13 ft wide and had 12 oars. The *Alfred Cory* was Southwold's third lifeboat and the last sailing one. In forty-one launchings, it saved forty-seven lives. There is a model in Southwold church and the top of the flag-pole was used as a weather vane. The Southwold lifeboat station was established during the 1850s.

SOUTHWOLD LIFEBOAT MEN, 1925, at the front of the lifeboat shed, Ferry Road. Back row, left to right: Joe Palmer, Binks Palmer, Bludgeon Palmer, Worky Upcraft, Johnny Critton, ? Albany. Middle row: B. Stanard, A. Stanard, C. Stanard, Erno May, Black Jack Palmer, Criss Stanard. Front row: Jack Herrington, S. Ashmenhall, Frank Upcraft, Mrs Horsfall, Hobbs Mayhew, E.R. Cooper (secretary).

LANDING SPRATS at Southwold c. 1925. Pier Pavilion is in the background. The longshore boats landed hundreds of bushels of sprats. The beach fishermen relied on the sprat fishing to provide them with a living. About 300 men and boys were engaged in fishing off Southwold Beach in 1900. 'At Swole or Southole, they cure sprats in the same manner as they do at Yarmouth: ... they make sprats red,' wrote Defoe in 1724.

FISHER GIRLS at Southwold Harbour, November 1910. Large numbers of Scots girls used to arrive for the herring season.

SOUTHWOLD HARBOUR, 1906. Work starts on harbour construction; there was no quay at this point. The idea was to establish a fishery.

PACKING HERRINGS AT SOUTHWOLD HARBOUR, C. 1908.

THE FISH MART at Southwold Harbour, known locally as the Kipperdrome. It stood on the site of the present caravan park. In the photograph the road is being constructed. The market was built sometime between 1906 and 1911 when the fish trade at Southwold was enjoying a revival, taking the overflow from Lowestoft and Yarmouth. The Harbour declined during the First World War.

FISHERMEN AT WALBERSWICK. In the seventeenth century Walberswick's chief trade, apart from fishing, was in butter, cheese and wool to London in small coasters. In the mid-nineteenth century Walberswick had a quay for vessels of 100 tons. In summer the fishermen trawled for plaice, sole and skate. Drift nets were used in autumn for herring and sprats – the sprats were also used as bait for cod. In the church is a plaque to the memory of drowned fishermen.

ALDEBURGH. The cod smack, *Lady Montefiore*, owned by Tom War, 1901.

THE SPRATS AT ALDEBURGH, C. 1912. Left to right, Curley, Smith, Jim Cadle, –?–. About 200 people were engaged in fishing off the Aldeburgh beach around 1900. In 1843 Aldeburgh had about 200 licensed fishing boats, and sole and lobster was taken in great abundance, as well as herring and sprats, which were salted and dried for Holland, London and other markets. To celebrate a successful season, Aldeburgh sprat fishermen used to hold a special dinner at Christmas time. In the 1980s there were about twenty-five licensed fishing boats.

FISHING BOATS ON ALDEBURGH BEACH, c. 1912. Left to right: ? Easter, C. Mann, ? Cook, C. Burwood, –?– , –?–.

ALDEBURGH FISHER AND LIFEBOAT MAN. Note the medal.

ALDEBURGH LIFEBOAT, the *Aldeburgh* (1890–1899), with crew. Launched 54 times, it saved 152 lives. The cost of £374 was an anonymous gift. There were private lifeboats in the eighteenth and early nineteenth centuries. The Aldeburgh lifeboat station was established in 1824. In the late nineteenth century there were two lifeboat disasters. The *Pasco* capsized with the loss of three men and in 1899 the *Aldeburgh* capsized and seven of her crew were lost.

ALDEBURGH LIFEBOAT, the *City of Winchester* (1902–1928). Launched forty-three times, it saved forty lives. Cost £2,640.

HIGH TIDE AT ALDEBURGH, 1938.

HIGH TIDE at Aldeburgh, 1938. A house on Fort Green has gone. In 1779 eleven houses went in one day.

THE *IONA*. In 1872 the *Iona* was made into a boathouse, but eventually rotted and was burnt. At the end of the nineteenth century a company of fishermen bought six derelict trawlers. The trawlers were towed from Lowestoft up the river to Slaughden and berthed on the saltings by an exceptionally high spring tide.

SLAUGHDEN, c. 1910, showing the Mariners inn in the background. Ships were once built at Slaughden and there were warehouses near the inn. A soap factory was established. In the latter part of the nineteenth century there were 100 fishing boats and 25 coasters. The inn, the warehouses and most of Slaughden were taken by the hungry sea.

SEA HARVEST. Scots girls gutting herrings at Southwold in 1908.

SECTION NINE

Land

I am thankful I was born early enough to hear the rumble of harvest wagons . . .

I am glad to have forked sheaves . . .

Now I see the rare rhythms of their work, building a round stack . . . What instinct, what an eye for form they hạd . . . But who can transport to paper the quiet of their strenuous farming days, or the rhythm of the tread of a dozen horses in plough-trace or shafts, which governed the rhythm of the farm? Or recall its chime of small sounds – ting of pail, spud scraping plough breast, clang of rib-roll, chains jangling as a team swung homeward at the end of the day?

Adrian Bell

A SUFFOLK DUN COW, from a print published in 1802. The Suffolk Dun had a great reputation as a milch cow. In the early nineteenth century some farmers started crossing the breed with the Norfolk horned cattle to produce a dual purpose animal. By the mid-nineteenth century the two breeds had merged into one, the Red Poll.

DRAUGHT BULLOCKS at Hazlewood, near Aldeburgh, c. 1900, with Amos Wilson of Aldeburgh, who always used three bullocks for ploughing and harrowing. The ruins are of a church known as St Mary's. The records of the Borough of Aldeburgh, 15 May 1476 state that, 'Agnes Leaves of Aldeburgh leaves in her will Twelve pence to the High Altar at Hazlewood.'

PLOUGHING WITH HORSES with what looks like an old Suffolk wooden swing plough. Sheep are grazing in the background. The ploughman has stopped, probably to pose for the camera, as the traces are slack and the swingle-trees are lying on the ground. The date and location of this photograph, like others in this section, are unknown but it would probably have been taken around 1900.

SUFFOLK PUNCHES ploughing at Firs Farm, Friston, c. 1937. The ploughman is Fred Driver. The colour of the Suffolk horse is chesnut (with only one 't') and it is clean-legged. The breed dates back to 1506. Every animal now in existence traces its descent in the direct male line to a horse foaled in 1760. It was said that the main difference between the Shire and the Suffolk was that the former knew when it had a load beyond its power to move but that the Suffolk would go on trying.

BROADCASTING SEED. The seed container was called a sid lip. The men, experts at broadcasting seed, were amazingly accurate, covering the ground evenly and sowing the seed to within a few pounds per acre. The broadcast seed would later be covered with earth by means of harrows.

SOWING CORN SEED with a Smyth swing drill made at Peasenhall. One man drove the team of horses and another attended to the drill behind. These drills were very accurate in sowing seed.

MOWING GRASS FOR HAY. This was a hard task for horses as the machine was powered by land wheel and thus by the horses. Mowing was usually done early in the morning as the grass cut easier when damp with dew and later the sun became too hot for the horses to work in comfort.

HOEING TURNIPS, C. 1910–1915. Hoeing is essential for getting a good crop, said Arthur Young, a Suffolk man and the first Secretary to the Board of Agriculture. He recommended feeding turnips to sheep on the land (folding) as the best preparation for growing barley. William Cobbett remarked upon the huge amount of turnips in Suffolk.

HAYSEL at Blythburgh in the 1920s or '30s. The hay is in cocks to give some protection from the weather and to facilitate picking it up and pitching on the cart. The magnificent church, 127 ft long and 54 ft wide, is an indication of the former size and importance of Blythburgh. During a service on 4 August 1577 'a strange and terrible tempest' struck the church. Lightning caused the spire to tumble down through the roof, shattering the font, killing a man and boy and scorching several members of the congregation. 'Blythburgh,' wrote Julian Tennyson, 'stands on a knoll beside the river; in the midst of a great ocean of marsh and heath, brooding graciously over the small cottages, that are the pitiable relics of a once wealthy port.'

FARSES, FOURSES OR BEEVERS, c. 1900. The afternoon break for refreshments in the days before farming became dehumanized and when work produced a sense of community, when men could talk and laugh as they worked. Note the men's hobnailed boots, sometimes called 'honky donks' or 'high lows'. This farm was only 150 acres but employed a far, far larger staff than a farm of the same size today.

HARVEST GANG. Men travelled from farm to farm cutting corn at so much per acre. A good scythesman could cut two acres per day, but the days were long and arduous. Some men worked on the land during the summer and went to sea during the winter, and were called 'half and halfers'. Note the horn, bow or cradle attached to the scythes to catch the falling crop, and the variety of hats. In their hands are 'rubs', used to sharpen the scythes.

CUTTING CORN WITH BINDER AND HORSES. Two or three teams would be used in turn, each working for a period of about two hours. The binder worked continuously throughout the day and, as the machine was powered by land wheel, it was arduous work for horses.

CUTTING CORN WITH BINDER AND TRACTOR. A man sits on the binder to make any necessary adjustments and to see that everything is in order.

HARVESTING at the Scarlett's farm at Westleton a few years later, but this time with combine harvesters. Note the good crop of wheat, and this before the use of large amounts of artificial fertilizers and chemical sprays.

THE SCARLETT FAMILY in the harvest field at Westleton, c. 1944. The Standard Fordson tractor on the left has iron wheels with spade lugs on the rear wheels.

HARVESTING IN THE OLDER STYLE at Reydon in 1934. Many of the beautiful old wagons such as this were later hitched behind tractors and rattled to death. In the foreground are stooks of corn, called 'shocks' in Suffolk.

MR ALFRED MOYES, the first man to drive a tractor in Reydon, c. 1920. After forty years with horses he was shown the tractor and told, 'There, off you go!' At first he still shouted 'Whoa!' when approaching a ditch, then had to fetch his horses to pull the tractor out of the ditch. The tractor is a Wallace which only had one front wheel. Behind are the sails of a binder.

THRESHING WITH A STEAM TRACTION ENGINE. The corn stack is to the left of the threshing machine, the straw elevator and straw stack to the rear, and sacks are being filled at the front. Note the sheet on top to keep wind from the men cutting sheaf bonds and feeding sheaves into the machine. This was a dirty, dusty job. Threshing tackle went from farm to farm during the winter, before the combines, which did harvesting and threshing in one operation, arrived.

Windmills

Gone with the wind
Ernest Dowson

THE CORN MILL at Walberswick, c. 1900.

DUNWICH ROAD, WESTLETON. A post-mill built before 1811 by Collins of Ipswich. Note the fly (a fantail) which brought the sails into the wind. This is said to be the prototype of Friston Mill. Timber from the demolished mill now forms the post for the village sign which has one of the millstones at its foot.

MIDDLETON. The post on which the buck in a post-mill revolves is supported by a trestle of four quarter bars. The base timbers are raised on brick piers.

TOWER MILL, THEBERTON, partially demolished in the mid-1920s. Tower mills are built of brick and are usually round. Unlike post-mills it is not necessary for the whole structure to turn because the sails are fitted to a cap or gable. In this photograph the fly can be seen on the cap.

SAXMUNDHAM. The brick roundhouse is now a petrol filling station.

PEASENHALL. The remains of another mill.

DARSHAM, c. 1933. The top was later taken down and the mill converted to oil power.

SMOCK MILL, LEISTON, covered with boards and, as was usual, octagonal. As with the tower mill only the cap revolves. Red Poll cattle, the native breed of Suffolk, are in the foreground. The cattle are renowned for thriftiness, hardiness and longevity. The bullocks make excellent beef and the cows produce economic and sensible yields, an ideal breed for the general farmer which unjustly lost favour.

FRISTON MILL in 1933, built in 1811 to 1812, a typical Suffolk post-mill. It was 55 ft in height and reputed to be the tallest in England. It had three pairs of millstones, and as business increased another set of millstones and an oat roller were set up in the Mill House. Until 1908 these were driven by a Garrett portable steam engine. It is probable that Friston Mill was built by John Collins of Ipswich. In 1875, during a severe thunderstorm, one of the stocks broke and a pair of sails crashed to the ground. In 1943 it happened again, and from then until 1955 the mill worked with only one pair of sails. After 1955 an engine was used to drive the mill. This mill is still standing and further restoration is being planned by Mr Hartley, the present owner.

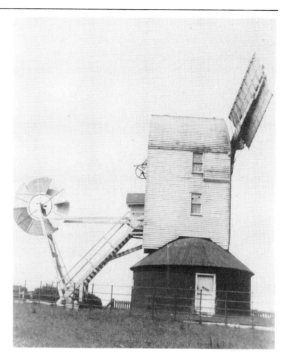

ALDRINGHAM MILL, 1919. This mill was moved to Thorpeness in 1922 or '23.

THE ALDRINGHAM MILL at Thorpeness, seen from the House in the Clouds. The mill post was drilled all the way through and converted to a wind pump to supply Thorpeness with water.

HUDSON'S MILL, SNAPE. The top was removed and the roundhouse converted into a house by Benjamin Britten, c. 1937.

MASKIN'S MILL, SNAPE. An open treble mill with common sails made of canvas.

STATION MILL, ALDEBURGH in the 1930s, just before fishermen started to pull it down.

THE MILL ON FORT GREEN, Aldeburgh. An ordinary brick tower mill. The tower remains and has been converted into a house.

ACKNOWLEDGEMENTS

Photographs loaned by:

Adnams Brewery ● D. Banthorpe ● R. Collett ● J. Denny ● Dunwich Museum
Mrs Gissing ● W. Greer ● P. Kett ● Long Shop Museum
Middleton Community Council ● D. Moyse ● D. Oliver ● J. Smith
J. Tooke ● Westleton Community Council ● R. Wright.